To

Wm. Reed Jerome

with the compliments

of the Author

July 1863

Your Loving Son
Willie—

MEMORIAL

OF

WILLIAM KIRKLAND BACON,

LATE

ADJUTANT

OF THE

TWENTY-SIXTH REGIMENT OF NEW YORK STATE
VOLUNTEERS.

BY HIS FATHER.

UTICA, N. Y.
ROBERTS, PRINTER, 60 GENESEE STREET.
1863.

How sleep the brave, who sink to rest,
By all their country's wishes blest;
When spring, with dewy fingers cold,
Returns to deck their hallowed mould,
She there shall dress a sweeter sod
Than fancy's feet have ever trod.

By fairy hands their knell is rung,
By forms unseen their dirge is sung;
There HONOR comes a pilgrim gray,
To bless the turf that wraps their clay,
And FREEDOM shall awhile repair
To dwell a weeping hermit there.

COLLINS.

ADJUTANT BACON.

I PROPOSE to erect a simple memorial, inscribing thereon the name of my departed son. It is a debt due to his memory, which some one should discharge, and who better than the father that knew and loved him. If I needed a warrant for this, I might plead even high authority. I remember more than forty years ago, to have read with great admiration, and with much youthful sensibility, the memoir prepared by the poet Beattie, of a son of brilliant promise cut off in the morning of life, and passages of that moving tribute now, at the distance of nearly half a century, still linger in my memory; and every admirer of Burke will readily recall that heart-broken wail over an only son, dearly loved and early lost, which will live as long as the unequaled orations that have made his name immortal. I do not of course venture to compare my case with these signal and affecting instances, but I use them by way of illustration, or better still, perhaps, of apology for my attempt.

Much, under these circumstances, must of course

A*

be pardoned—and will be by the feeling and the charitable—to the paternal heart sorely wounded, and parental hopes shattered and crushed, but I still think with President Stearns, who has given to us an admirable portraiture of a son of the finest promise and most devoted heroism, the Adjutant of a Massachusetts regiment, who gave his life for his country at Newbern, that "if proper allowance is made for parental partiality and tenderness, perhaps, in the case of one so early called away, no person could give a better impression of his real life and motives than his father."

I approach the task with no desire or expectation of making a sensation, or bequeathing a name to posterity. Fame is nothing to him now who sleeps quietly with kindred dust on Forest Hill, and less than nothing to me, who have buried so many hopes and aspirations in his early grave. For friendly eyes, and gentle and loving, as well as manly hearts, not lost to tenderness, while they kindle with admiration, this brief record is intended.

William Kirkland Bacon, the only son of William Johnson and Eliza Kirkland Bacon, was born at Utica, N. Y., on the fifteenth day of February, 1842. He fell, mortally wounded, at the battle of Fredericksburgh, on the thirteenth day of December, 1862, and expired on the morning of the sixteenth of December, having just attained the age of twenty years and ten months.

His christian name was designed in part to perpetuate a family patronymic borne by the remotest ancestor of the family in England, of whom we have any certain knowledge, William Bacon, of Stretton, in Rutlandshire. His son, Hon. Nathaniel Bacon, a Councilman in the old Colony of Plymouth, the founder of the family on this side of the Atlantic, emigrated to this country, and settled in Barnstable, Mass., about the year 1640, a little less than twenty years after the landing of the Pilgrims at Plymouth. The whole name commemorated one very dear to us, his uncle WILLIAM KIRKLAND, one of the best and truest and kindest-hearted of men, who died many years ago, greatly lamented by his family, his friends, and, indeed, by all who knew him.

Of ancestral distinction, if such should happen to exist, it is not worth while for any one in this country, and under our institutions, to speak. Of the progenitors of my son, whether near or remote, I have nothing more to say than that they were plain and independent and honest men, who served their generation faithfully, as I believe, both in private and in public life, and were all loyal and true to the government they upheld and the country they loved. This may be emphatically said of two, at least, in the line of ascent, his great-grandfather, JOHN BACON, of Stockbridge, Mass., and his venerable grandfather, EZEKIEL BACON, who at the advanced age of nearly eighty-seven, still survives to honor the memory of a loyal grandson. Both of them wore the unsullied ermine of the Judge, and both were called into the service of the country, and took part in the State and National councils in stirring and critical times. The former witnessed the rebellion of Shays in 1786, and actually took the field on the side of the Government, and assisted in the capture and dispersion of a band of rebels in the County of Berkshire, and the restoration of the supremacy of law and order in the good old Commonwealth. The latter was in Congress in 1812, and onwards, and subsequently in the Treasury Department, and was among the most earnest and active supporters of the Government during that period that tried the patriotism and the spirit of our public men.

Upon the side both of his father and mother, the latter a daughter of the late Gen. JOSEPH KIRKLAND, "*clarum et venerabile nomen*," WILLIAM was a descendant of the Pilgrims, and Puritan blood, better than the fabled "ichor" of the heathen deities, ran in his veins. And of this blood, thank God, he was not, as he had no reason to be, ashamed. It is the fashion just now, among scheming and time-serving politicians, and empty-headed bigots, who ignore history and live upon tradition, to depreciate and decry the Pilgrim fathers, and impugn the sincerity of their descendants. We can afford to smile at this, remembering how secure the past is, and how certain the future will be to vindicate the memory of the descendants of men of whom the old world "was not worthy." When we recall the fact that the tory Hume was constrained to confess that to the Puritans, England owed all the freedom of her Constitution, and repeat, with an exulting sense of its truthfulness, the glowing eulogy of Macaulay, we may be consoled, nay, grow proud and jubilant, that our life-blood tracks its parent lake to such a source. If there are any in this community who are ashamed to own their origin, and with unfilial hand smite the dear mother that bore, or nourished them, let them go out from us, for doubtless "they are not of us," nor of any companionship such as true and honorable men alone will covet.

I shall spend no time upon the infancy or boyhood of my son. There was nothing remarkable about him in those early days, and but slight foundation for the erection of those airy castles that parents not unfrequently build, baseless and unsubstantial as most of them are. This should perhaps be said, that anterior to, and especially succeeding his birth, the state of his mother's health, owing to nervous prostration, was such that it might almost be said, in Byron's words, that he was

> "Born in grief, and nurtured in convulsion,"

although eminently a "child of love." I allude to this, however, only to add that this fact drove his mother, with a constraining, agonizing grasp, to take fast hold on the Divine covenant, and with almost ceaseless prayers and tears to give her child away to God from the moment of his birth; a dedication renewed and reiterated with pangs of maternal tenderness and the exercise of strong Christian faith, from that hour to the day of his death.

I pause only at this period of his life to say, that he passed through the usual course of instruction in the schools for the young, and in our excellent Common Schools and Free Academy, making no special mark, but taking a fair rank both as to scholarship and deportment. In his early days he was under the charge, for a year or more, of one young lady, a dear and valued friend of his mother, who took special interest in him, and impressed her own sweet nature upon his more mercurial and impulsive temperament, to a degree that I think left its footprints to some extent on all his future life. The year preparatory to his entering College, he spent in the family and under the judicious instruction of the Rev. JONATHAN EDWARDS WOODBRIDGE, of Auburndale, Mass. It was a happy and profitable year to him, and he secured a very kind and faithful friend in his excellent teacher. Of the esteem in which he was held by him, I have good evidence in a letter recently received from Mr. W., in which he says, "I do not think I ever had a pupil in my school that I loved as I did WILLIE, my own son excepted. I hoped he was to pass through the war safely, and that I was to have the satisfaction of seeing, and rejoicing with him, after it was all over. He was to me almost as a son. It gives me a melancholy pleasure to learn that he developed so manly and gallant a character—melancholy, because these and other noble qualities with which he was endowed, are lost so soon to the world."

He entered Hamilton College in the fall of 1859, and remained there till the month of April, 1861, when his substantial life may be said to have commenced; and the record of all that is essential may be embraced within the short ensuing period of twenty months. His general scholarship was not at all above the ordinary level, but he took a good position and perhaps attained some little distinction as a classical student, some memorials of which have been preserved by one who was his instructor mainly in this department of his studies, Prof. EDWARD NORTH, a man who was high in his regard, and of whom he always spoke in those endearing terms that a warm personal friendship inspires. One instance of his scholarly taste and attainments was brought to notice after his death, by an article in the paper, which was readily traced to Professor North; and upon a suggestion to him, that notice has been slightly elaborated, and a communication made to me, which I have taken the liberty to annex in a note in the Appendix.*

He was quietly pursuing his allotted tasks, when the guns of Sumpter startled the country like the shock of an earthquake. His parents and

* See note A.

friends, in common with all the loyal at the North, keenly felt the blow the honor and integrity of the country had received. The son of their affections had not, with heedless ears and vacant mind, heard the instructions that from his earliest years had taught him love of liberty, loyalty to rightful authority, and fidelity to conscience. He heard the trumpet call of our honest and fearless Chief Magistrate, and his spirit with a bound leaped upon the ramparts where the great cause was to be defended, and the great wrong and dishonor redressed. He at once came home, and presented his earnest plea to be allowed to go forth and enroll himself in any capacity among the defenders of his country and her glorious flag. With some struggles, in which nature and duty held stern contest, the consent of his father was first gained, coupled however with the indispensable condition that not without a mother's assent and blessing should he go forth. It was filially and reverently sought, and by both parent and child the question was, upon the bended knee and in earnest supplication, committed to God. An hour of communion with Him resulted in the strongest conviction that duty required the sacrifice of all private and personal considerations to the call of the country, and the victim, if such he was to be, was laid upon the altar, never more to be regretted—never to be recalled.

He enrolled himself as a private in Company A, of the now famous Fourteenth Regiment of New York Volunteers, being the first company of the first regiment that Oneida County sent forth to the defense of the Government in the hour of its peril. With his company he went to Washington, arriving there on or about the seventeenth of June, 1861, and immediately went into camp. About this time he was invited by Col. Christian, of the Twenty-Sixth Regiment New York Volunteers, to take a position as his Military Clerk; and in order to effect his transfer, I went to Washington in July, and completed the arrangement by which he became a private in that regiment, the noble Twenty-Sixth, which amid many discouragements and under some adverse circumstances, has seen as much hard service, endured as many privations uncomplainingly, stood as bravely and lost perhaps as heavily in battle as any regiment this State has sent into the field. It has rarely, if ever, been mentioned in official dispatches, and received but a scant measure of commendation from any other quarter; but when its thinned and more than decimated ranks shall come back to their homes, (alas! that so many homes shall welcome no more the loved ones they sent forth,) their true merit will be appreciated, and the hard-earned laurels they have won will not be denied to them.

I spent four or five days with him in Washington, and in visiting the camps and forts in the region around. Among other scenes of interest we witnessed a dress parade of two Rhode Island regiments, then under the command of Colonel Burnside, since the distinguished Commander-in-Chief of the Army of the Potomac; and were at the time much impressed with his unpretending, yet manly and soldier-like bearing. We were present at their evening service, and heard the voices of nearly two thousand men, as with uncovered heads, beneath the blue canopy, they united in sacred song, when the stars seemed to look lovingly down upon them;

> "And the sounding aisles of the dim woods rang
> To the Anthem of the Free."

I left him cheerful, contented and happy, in the hope of soon seeing active service. He did not realize his expectation then, although the battle of Bull Run was fought within three days after I left him. His regiment had not been sent forward with the army to that fatal field; but immediately on the retreat of our forces, it was ordered to advance to the rescue and support of our shattered columns, arrest the tide of retreat, and if need be drive back the invaders. Among the troops that formed a part of the army of McDowell on that occasion, was the Seventy-First Regiment, from the City of New York, in which his two cousins, Edward and Charles Kirkland had gone forward as privates. The latter had been his playmate and companion from infancy, and between them there existed a friendship akin to that of David and Jonathan; a love indeed it might with almost as much truth be said, "passing the love of women." Before the Twenty-Sixth advanced into Virginia, the dismal tidings of defeat came pouring into our camps, with of course a thousand exaggerations; and, among the rest, that the New York Seventy-First had been all cut up and destroyed. On the eve of marching over, WILLIE addressed a brief letter to his mother, announcing the service upon which they were going, giving a hurried account of the rout and retreat, and the terrible slaughter, as reported, of our troops. "The Seventy-First," he says, "is horribly cut up. Poor, dear Charlie, I fear, has gone to his long, long home, and Ned, too, as well. Perhaps it may be my lot to follow them soon. We shall probably be on the advance this time, as our regiment is to take the post of honor and of danger on the right. I do not expect that I shall be spared. It seems to me as if I could not bear to live any longer, except for your sake, if dear Charlie is really killed. You know how great our love was for each other, and can not be surprised that I should feel as I do." He closes the letter thus: "To-day I go on. I hope that if I fall I may be forgiven all my sins, past and present, and be taken home to God. Strange as it may seem, I do not dread death much. When I think of it, I can not give myself up to gloomy forebodings. I only pray and hope. You, too, will pray for me, dear mother. With a heart brimful of love for you and every body, I remain your loving son."

The advance was only made as far as Fairfax, and as no enemy appeared to encounter, the regiments ordered forward saw no service, and soon returned to their former positions. It turned out also, to his great joy, that both his cousins were unharmed, Charlie having, through illness, been by his commanding officer compelled to leave the ranks before the regiment reached the field, and Edward having borne himself gallantly through the fight, coming off unscathed.

All remember the weary weeks and months of

inaction that followed, while the army was reorganizing under the admirable drill and discipline of McClellan, which the country long hoped and expected would be followed by some sudden and signal success. But no movement took place, and the succeeding winter and spring was spent by the Twenty-Sixth mainly in constructing and garrisoning forts Lyon and Ellsworth, in the neighborhood of Alexandria; a life the tedium of which was relieved by very little of incident or adventure of any kind. In the month of August, 1861, an agitation arose in the regiment in regard to the term of their enlistment; and it seemed likely to breed a serious disturbance, unless promptly checked. The Colonel called about him his officers, and stated that he desired none to remain except such as were prepared to serve the full two years. Upon this, fourteen officers tendered their resignations, which were at once accepted, and their successors, from among those who were "in for the war," selected, and their names sent to the Governor of New York. With the promptness and courtesy that always distinguished Governor Morgan, the new commissions were immediately issued, and delivered to my son, who returned with them to the camp without revisiting his home. Among the new appointments,

WILLIE was named for Adjutant of the regiment, a position he modestly, yet promptly accepted, and was at once commissioned, and continued in that post until his death, discharging its duties, as I have occasion to know, with great fidelity, and in a manner to gain the entire respect of his superior officers, and the love and confidence of the men.

As soon as our son left home, a correspondence at once commenced between his family and friends and himself; sustained mainly on our side by his mother and sister. The number of letters that passed between us on both sides amount to some three hundred, and they form a most striking and touching record of our mutual joys, trials, hopes and anxieties during that short but eventful period. The recent perusal of this correspondence, has re-opened many sealed fountains, and awakened that "mighty hunger of the heart," not to be satisfied by any thing this side of Heaven. I do not intend to dwell on this at any length, but I propose to extract some passages from his letters at various dates, but without particular order, and chiefly to illustrate two points having reference to the principle and the spirit with which he entered on and persevered in the service of his country, and the glimpses they afford of his interior life and religious impressions, so far as he manifested them. They were written for no eyes but ours, with no possible thought of publicity, upon which he put a stern interdict, and are now re-produced only for the gratification of his friends, who would like to think of him as he was, a true patriot though a beardless boy, with a soul of honor, a personal purity unsullied, and a conscience, as I humbly but confidently believe, "void of offense towards God and towards man."

In May, 1861, he wrote as follows: "I have no doubt God is on our side. We are contending against principles the most subversive of every law, human and divine. We are contending for the most sacred privileges granted to man—for the maintenance of liberty, civilization and humanity. In such a contest God will give the victory to the cause in which our fathers fought, and who were, by his favor, successful. I feel as if nothing was too much to give in behalf of so glorious a cause; and if it is decreed that I shall fall, be assured, dear mother, that my life will be a willing sacrifice. I only hope and pray that I may be prepared to die." In the month of June he gave to his sister, very fully, his views of camp life, and the causes which tended to demoralization in the army. The life of the soldier, when inactive, he says, "is lazy and shiftless in the extreme, and its effect demoralizing to the last degree, unless one's principles are firmly grounded and adhered to. The idea I had was that we should march right on to bear the brunt of battle, and at the expiration of about a year return home covered with glory and honor, or die a patriot's death. The probability however is that little fighting will be done, and we shall lie around this city to protect it." He concludes by saying, "Do not fear for me. My patriotism is as strong as ever. Although I am in the midst of temptations, rest assured, dear sister, that my honor and integrity shall be preserved intact. I shall combat with all my strength the attacks of those who would tempt me to mingle in any kind of vice, iniquity or wrong-doing." And this resolution he carried with him to the end, and by the grace of God it was his shield and buckler, which warded off "all the fiery darts of the wicked."

During the summer the regiment was without any adequate religious aid or instruction; and it was not until the month of October, 1861, that their excellent Chaplain, the Rev. Dr. D. W. Bristol, received his appointment, and went on to the regiment. I need hardly say that his influence, so far as it was allowed to operate, was most happy and beneficent. Between him and the Adjutant there forthwith sprung up a warm personal attachment; the plans and efforts of the Chaplain found in him a ready coadjutor, and confidence in each other and mutual regard continued to the end of WILLIE'S life. Writing to his mother, in July, 1861, he laments the desecration of the Sabbath, contrasting it with the quiet and peaceful scenes he had enjoyed at home, and adding, "I have hardly been alone enough to read my Bible, and when I do read, it seems as if every body swore and cursed more than ever, and took peculiar pains to disturb me. Nevertheless I manage to read as often as possible, and find great relief in its sacred pages." Again he says, in a letter a week later, "Another Sunday has come and gone, and how unlike the pleasant Sabbaths at home. There is no good Mr. Knox to preach to us. All the religious exercises of the day consisted in reading the articles of war, and a benediction by the Chaplain. I often think of the contrast between the Sabbaths here, and those quiet, lovely Sabbaths at Auburndale, where every thing and every body seemed to observe the holy day. You would hardly hear a discordant sound there, but here all is otherwise."

In this same month of July his venerable

grandmother departed this life. He was of course unable to be present at the funeral obsequies, and was advised by letter of the circumstances of her departure. He had always been a favorite grandchild, and he sincerely mourned her loss. In response to our letters, he wrote as follows: "I was very much grieved to hear of dear grandma's death. * * * * I never can forget her dear face. I seem to see it even now, and can not fully realize I shall never see her again. She was very dear to me. When I read your letter and knew that she was gone forever from the world, I could not keep back the tears. It seemed childish, but was much less than her memory deserved. * * * * Her death led me into a train of serious reflection. It caused me to think of the unblemished name which has always been sustained by both sides of my family, and I have determined *never* to be recreant in maintaining, as far as I am concerned, the spotless integrity of my ancestors, which has been so well preserved for many generations. Won't you, dear mother, just to oblige me, plant some little flower on her grave, a forget-me-not, or something of that kind? *Perhaps I may be the next to be laid by her side.* No one can fathom the mysteries of the Divine dispensations. I hope I may be prepared for whatever fate awaits me. You, I know, will pray for me, and I try to do so for myself. Though I fear I am far from being a Christian, I hope I shall be found worthy of Heaven when I die." How strangely prophetical does that italicized sentence sound, read in the light of the fact that his form was the next to be laid in the ground where his grandmother sleeps. Did "coming events" in this, as in the closing hours of his life, "cast their shadows before?"

In August he wrote me a letter describing a night adventure in which he, with his warmly-attached friend Captain Arrowsmith, performed a humble, but as they supposed a very useful service, and closing thus: "When one sees how much the country needs his services at this crisis, can he, with any degree of self-satisfaction, consent to return home, however much he would love to see once more those whom he has left behind? For my own part, sooner than leave the service of my country, to which I am indebted for the blessings of unbounded freedom, I would consent to die the worst of deaths. Our country is now passing through a terribly trying ordeal, but I hope she will come out purified by the test. God is on our side, and by his help we will crush out the hydra-headed monster of disunion, and I hope settle once and for all the agitating question of slavery."

In the fall he had the pleasure of welcoming his kind friend the Chaplain, and on the fifth of November he tells his mother, "Dr. Bristol is here, and has preached to us. He has already become very popular in the regiment, and I am sure will be just the man for us. Last Sunday he held a temperance meeting in the afternoon, and a prayer meeting in the evening, besides the regular morning service, and very interesting meetings they were; doubly so to me, as they reminded me of home, and all the social and religous advantages I enjoyed there. I have no doubt he will be a great blessing to the regiment." The expressions in this letter are a sample of many others of similar import which occur throughout his correspondence, and denote the estimation in which he held the Chaplain and his services.

I could multiply extracts of this character, but these will suffice. I close with a pleasant allusion to his home, which he visited but once during his long absence, until brought back after his wound at Manassas, but which was often in his thoughts in his weary marches and more weary watchings: "I think of you all," he says, in March, 1862, "every day, and long for the time when I may return to my dear family. It may be a long time before I do, but I can not help a sort of home-sickness occasionally. 'There's no place like home.'" And alluding to some little remembrance his mother had sent him, he adds: "How kind and thoughtful you are, dear mother. You must not make so many sacrifices for my sake, for it will not take long to make the debt of gratitude I owe you infinitely greater than I can ever hope to pay."

In the month of July, 1862, the active service the regiment had been so impatiently waiting for, commenced. I do not propose to follow the long and harassing march of the regiment down to the Rappahannock, back again to Manassas, then to Front Royal, then again to Warrenton, and then the retreat under Pope, until they reached again the old and fatal field of Manassas, in the vicinity of which the second discomfiture took place, on the thirtieth of August. In this battle my son received his first wound. His account of this has been read by a few of his friends, but is of sufficient interest, perhaps, to bear repetition in part.

BAPTIST CHURCH HOSPITAL,
Alexandria, September 3, 1862.

* * * * "We came up in beautiful style by the flank, amidst a shower of shot and shell, and

were ordered to a hill on the left of the left center, to support the 5th Maine Battery, which was being placed in position. The gunners had just unlimbered and loaded when the regiment in front broke, and came running towards the battery. Before the battery had time to fire on the rebels, they were within five rods of it. The gunners delivered one fire right in the face of the enemy, then turned with the horses and caissons, and ran straight into our ranks, while the broken regiments rushed upon us at the same time. The right of the regiment, where my place is, had not yet broken, but turning to the left, I saw our colors, the old stars and stripes, retiring before the enemy. Immediately after the left and center broke, however, the right, too, turned and fled. You can imagine my feelings at this moment. Mortification, shame, indignation, were all commingled. I turned my horse's head, and called to the men not to run, and by word and gesture, as well as action, endeavored to stop them. The officers succeeded at last in rallying the colors and about two hundred men, and for a while we made a desperate stand, although flanked on the left, and subjected to a most severe and deadly fire, completely enfilading us. Finally the men were forced to retire, mostly in disorder, but some in squads still firing on the enemy. Capt. Palmer with five men was making a last gallant stand, near the left of the 94th New York, and I was standing by cheering the men on as well as I knew how, when suddenly, amidst the peculiar whistle of the Minie balls, I heard a quick "thug," and felt a very sharp pain in my left leg, just above the ankle. Looking down, I saw that I was wounded, how severely I could not tell. I tried to step on my left foot, but found the pain severe enough to prevent my bearing my full weight on that leg. Seeing that the regiment was now wholly disorganized, and my presence could be of no further avail, I walked backward from the field with my sword still drawn and my face to the enemy, until I was entirely out of range, when I turned about and moved slowly away. The pain in my leg was gradually increasing, and falling in with the caissons of the 5th Maine Battery, I rode upon one of them for some distance. The road was so rough that I could not endure this long, and therefore I got off and inquired for a surgeon. All the surgeons were busy, however, and all the ambulances full. Just then I fell in with a corporal of our regiment, who gave me his assistance, and leaning on his arm I walked five miles, until I got an opportunity to ride in a transportation wagon. In this were two wounded men, and crawling over them, I laid down on the hay in the back of the wagon, and got a good rest for the night. In the morning I sent word to the Colonel, asking to be taken to our ambulances. The Colonel came, put me on his horse and carried me to our wagon train, but neither surgeons nor ambulances were to be found. I forgot to tell you that my horse was wounded in the neck, and became unmanageable while I was endeavoring to rally the regiment, and I dismounted, and let him run loose *supposing him to be mortally wounded; fortunately it* proved otherwise, for on my arrival at the wagon train I found him there. He had been caught by one of the boys while wandering around near the battle field. The Colonel had concluded that I was killed. On my horse I rode down to Alexandria, after trying in vain to obtain attention at Centerville, and here I am. I was able to hobble around quite well the other day, but yesterday, in consequence of using my leg too much, I was completely laid up, and forced to keep my bed. I am in the pleasantest hospital in town, close to the house of the postmaster, Mr. Massey, and am treated with the greatest kindness by his wife and daughters, with whom I became acquainted just before leaving Fort Lyon. Other good Union ladies have been to visit me and bring me delicacies, for which I am very grateful—though I don't feel the want of them so much now, after all. A "hard tack" and a cup of tea or coffee are all-sufficient for me, after becoming accustomed to long marches day after day, with nothing to eat."

This letter contained the first intelligence we had received of him since the battle, and I forthwith left for Washington, found him at the Hospital in Alexandria, cheerful and hopeful of an early recovery and return to the service, brought him to his home by easy stages, where he spent forty days among the happiest of his or of our life, received unnumbered kindnesses and compliments from friends, neighbors and companions, old and young, in regard to all which he was modest and reticent; and under the judicious counsel of Dr. Coventry, the assiduous and untiring attention of his dear friend Dr. Douglass, and the tender nursing of mother and sisters, he rapidly recovered. At the end of his furlough he tore himself away, not unwillingly, though not without some lingering looks at the home he left for the last time, to rejoin his regiment, on the twenty-second of last October. On reaching Washington he was examined by the Hospital Surgeon, and advised strongly against proceeding to his regiment for at least twenty days, his wound not then having closed; but such was his anxiety to be with his brethren and companions in the field, that he left the next morning for Harper's Ferry, and rejoined the regiment at Berlin, walking on that day six miles to overtake it.

It was a common remark among his friends, and was indeed noticeable in all his deportment, during this brief visit to his home, that in both physical and mental development, a great change had come over him. He had passed from the light-hearted and impulsive boy to the maturity of early manhood. His views of life and of his own position were greatly chastened as well as matured. The youthful enthusiasm that doubtless had to some extent inspired and influenced his original purpose, had given place to severe and stern reality; and his second return to the post of duty and of honor, was with a very sober and thoughtful view of the true condition of the country, and of his own responsibilities and probable exposure and peril. A suggestion casually made to him that he might honorably resign, was met with so emphatic and prompt a rejection, that it was never repeated, and the call again to the field of active duty seemed to him then more imperative than ever. In this light he looked steadily at the issue, and prepared himself with earnest resolution to encounter whatever the future had in store for him. The death of his cousin, Lieut. EDWARD THORNTON KIRKLAND, of Wisconsin, which occurred at the battle of Perryville, in September, greatly affected him. Edward was a gentle, but gallant boy, the only son of his mother, of nearly the same age with WILLIE, and between them there existed a warm friendship, and kindred impulses actuated both. He saw, perchance, in his, the shadow of his own impending fate. WILLIE had seven beloved cousins in the grand army of the Union, all thoroughly loyal and true to the government, some of whom have made a mark not to be forgotten by their friends or their countrymen, but Edward was the first to seal his devotion with his blood, so soon to be followed by him, the second martyr offered upon the holy shrine of freedom and humanity.

In a letter to his cousin, Julia Holley, written on the twenty-first of October, the day before he left home for the army, in allusion to this event,

WILLIE says: "Have you heard of the death of our noble cousin, Neddy Kirkland, Aunt Abby's son? He died as a cousin of ours should die, bravely fighting among the foremost of his comrades. I grieve for, and yet I glory in his death. God grant that I may never prove recreant."

His friends learned but little from his own lips respecting the part he had acted in the camp, on the march, or upon the battle field; and it was from others, and mostly from the privates in the ranks, that the incidents alluded to by President Fisher, in his funeral discourse, were gathered; and it was pleasant and gratifying to us to receive these unsought and voluntary testimonials. By the kindness of my friend George St. George, of Yorkville, who had maintained a correspondence with several soldiers of the gallant Twenty-Sixth, I was furnished with some letters addressed to him, from one of which, written in October, by John Williams, and relating especially to the battle of the thirtieth of August, I venture to make a brief extract: "We were going in by the left flank, and as soon as we came to a front, and before we had time to look around us, the first thing we saw was one of the regiments on top of the hill coming to about face, and tearing down the hill a little faster than the regulation allows for a double quick, running right into our left wing and breaking it, and a battery ran right through our right wing and broke that also; and by this time the rebels made their appearance on the top of the hill and opened on us. * * * Our color bearer was shot in the arm, and down came the flag, and just as I was going to pick it up, Paul McCluskey was ahead of me, and had the honor of taking it from the field. * * * All the men say that our Adjutant is the bravest man in the army. He fought like a lion at Bull Run, and all are very sorry that he was wounded, and I know that his good natured smile will be missed while he is gone. I hope he will be in the regiment when I get back again."

I resume the narrative. After overtaking the regiment, they marched, as is well known, after the army of Lee, down through Virginia and to the Rappahannock, which now again, and for the third time, they revisited. In all the campaigns in which they had been engaged, they had marched more than one thousand miles. Sickness, death, resignations, and desertion to some extent, had thinned its once full ranks, until at the end of this last journey the regiment numbered but little more than three hundred effective men. But what remained was "true as the steel of their tried blades;" and in the closing conflict, the record of their losses told the story of their bravery and endurance. The communications from my son were now infrequent, only five letters from him having reached us before the fatal battle of the thirteenth of December at Fredericksburgh. From Warrenton he wrote us on the tenth of November, that having received his horse from Washington soon after leaving Berlin, he had been able to get on very satisfactorily. "My wound," he says, "is only open as much as could be covered by a five cent piece, and the leg is in excellent condition. The next time I write I expect to be able to inform you that nothing is left of my wound save 'a pretty scar.'"

Then followed two hasty notes, advising us that his regiment was in the left grand division, under Franklin, in Reynolds' corps and Gibbons' division, and that a forward movement was daily and even hourly expected. He informed us also that some wretch had cut open his satchel, and stolen all his under clothing, leaving him almost literally nothing but the garments he stood in. Immediate preparations were made to supply his wants, and a package, carefully made up by diligent and loving hands, was entrusted to one who confidently expected within three days to deliver it. Enclosed within this package were the last loving words and faithful counsels of his mother. But the messenger lingered or was detained by the way, and only reached the banks of the Rappahannock on the afternoon of the thirteenth, after the dear boy for whom it was intended had received the fatal shot that rendered him thenceforth unconscious of a mother's tenderness, and only to be aided by her ceaseless prayers.

A hurried letter dispatched from his father by mail, came to his hands on the eve of the battle, and these were the last words he ever heard from home. His last letter to us was dated on the sixth of December. In it he alluded to some occurrences in the regiment which gave him some uneasiness, but he took occasion to add, "I don't say this because I am in the least disappointed on my own account. Promotion I never asked, or courted, or wished. I am satisfied to be where I am fitted to be, and where I can perform my duty honorably." It was strictly true that he had not asked promotion; on the contrary, when it was proposed to, and urged upon him, by our mutual friend, Hon. ROSCOE CONKLING, from whom he had received unnumbered kindnesses, and who estimated him, as he thought, altogether beyond his deserts, although the offer was most gratefully appreciated, it was firmly and persistently declined.

The last message he sent was one of earnest love to all at home, and the expression of a joyful expectation that in the ensuing month of May he would come back to us, having served out his time fully and honorably. The letter of his father closed with this sentence, the last that ever met his eyes from those he loved: "I sympathize with you, my dear son, in all your discomforts and distresses, and wish you were better situated. But you must do all that duty seems to require, and leave the results with God, to whom we daily commend you."

I approach the close of my simple story. On the twelfth of December, as is well known, the left grand division of the Army of the Potomac, under Franklin, crossed the Rappahannock, the Twenty-Sixth Regiment being in Gibbons' division, to which had been assigned the post of honor in the fierce assault which it had been determined the next day should witness, upon the entrenched position of the rebel army. That night the soldiers slept upon their arms, and orders had been passed to be ready for action at the earliest dawn. To the officers it was for the most part a night of sleeplessness and anxiety, and speculations as to the probable result of the operations of the ensuing day, were freely indulged. Among others, my son expressed his conviction that a terrible conflict was before them, to be attended by great loss of life, and that among the victims he would in all probability be numbered. In the gray twilight of the morning the regiment was roused from its uneasy repose, and by seven o'clock was all in order of battle, and ready for the advance. It took up its line of march towards the enemy, when a severe cannonade was opened upon them, and the whole division was ordered to cast itself upon the ground, while the balls and shells of the rebel batteries flew over them.

For many hours they thus remained in the wet and muddy bed which was their only resting place, and then in a lull of the storm, orders were given them to rise, advance and charge. All cheerfully and with alacrity took their places, and at this point occurred, as I understand, the repetition by my son to the commanding officer, Lieutenant Colonel Jennings, of his premonition of the fate impending over them, and the remark alluded to by Dr. Fisher in his funeral discourse. The rest is soon told. It was about the hour of three o'clock in the afternoon that the messenger of death reached him. In the confusion and excitement always attendant upon a battle field, it is difficult to attain much precision in details or results. According to one account, the Adjutant was at the extreme right, on foot, as were all the field officers, with his drawn sword cheering on the men. Another statement in the letter of a private of the Twenty-Sixth, says "he was in the thickest of the battle, and was seen to step in front of our line with a rifle, and shoot at the rebels, when he was struck;"—and another letter, written by John Sheean, a private in the Fiftieth New York, speaks as follows: "WILLIE BACON, the Adjutant, had one of his legs taken off, while gallantly leading on his regiment, loading and firing his rifle as fast as any man in the crowd. He cheered on his men all the time until he fell." The writer adds: "The men say some of their wounded were left on the field, but they say that if it had cost every man in the regiment to take WILLIE off, they would not have left him." The truth probably is, that either in the excitement of the moment, the "*certaminis gaudia*" which the true soldier feels, or for the purpose of encouragement to the men, he seized a rifle from the hand of one that had fallen, and commenced its discharge at the enemy. And this is rather confirmed by the fact that in the pocket of his coat were found, after his death, a handful of percussion caps and an undischarged rifle cartridge.

A Minie ball struck the front of the left leg, (the one that had previously been wounded,) in the upper third, passing entirely through the limb, and shattering the bone in its course. Uttering an exclamation, he fell at once to the ground. Orders definite and imperative had been given by the superior officers, that whoever fell during the fight, not a man must leave the ranks to render aid, or bear the wounded from the field, but all were to press on regardless of the wounded, the dying, or the dead. The then commanding officer of the regiment, (now Major Wetmore, of Yorkville, a man as humane as he is valiant,) saw WILLIE fall and two men spring to his assistance. He remembered the order, and strict discipline obliged him to enforce it, but he loved the Adjutant, and yielding to a natural impulse, he turned away from the scene, and affected not to see what if seen would have required from him official interposition to prevent. God bless him for his kind consideration and thoughtful obliviousness.

WILLIE was borne at once to the rear by Henry Clark and Thomas Welch, both privates in Company F, and soon placed in an ambulance with Captain Palmer, who was wounded nearly at the same time, and rapidly driven to and taken across the Rappahannock to the hospital previously prepared for the reception of the wounded. A message was sent that his case required instant attention, which at a glance his friend Dr. Walter B. Coventry also discovered, and forthwith the regimental, brigade and division surgeons were called to consult and decide upon the treatment he required. What occurred at this point, and subsequently, is better told in the words of Dr. ABRAHAM L. COX, the eminent surgeon attached to the brigade, than I could possibly relate it. My kind friend, the Rev. S. Hanson Coxe, the esteemed rector of Trinity Church, in Utica, addressed a letter to his uncle, soliciting from him a brief description of the circumstances attending the amputation. He complied in the most prompt and generous manner; and his communication is so satisfactory, and so replete with interest, that I print it in full in the Appendix.*

From the time the amputation was performed, on the evening of Saturday, the thirteenth of December, the sufferer lingered, mostly in a state of unconsciousness, and probably with very little pain, until about five o'clock on the morning of the sixteenth, when he quietly breathed his last.

* See note B.

He was, as Dr. Cox states, very uncomplaining, and made few exactions of those who kindly attended to his wants and watched over him. His faithful friend, the Chaplain, was frequently at his side, but from his great prostration and the wandering of his mind, was unable to hold any connected conversation with him, and could only commit him, as he repeatedly did, in silent but fervent prayer to his God and Saviour, the only and the great Physician who in that hour had power to help, and grace to support and to save in the moment of his extreme necessity.

The watchers who faithfully and tenderly cared for, and ministered to him, were Morris A. Brown, George Primmer, Edgar W. Seymour and William Cleminger, of the Drum Corps of the Twenty-Sixth Regiment. I record their names that I may associate them with the name that will ever live in my memory, and that my descendants may never forget them. From a letter of the last named to his father, written after WILLIE'S death, I am permitted to make the following extract: "We have lost another good friend to the Drum Corps, and a good and brave officer of the regiment, Adjutant BACON, son of Judge Bacon, of Utica. * * * * When the boys were bringing him off the field, he said he had fought his last battle; and so it proved. After his leg was taken off, he was light-headed most of the time, and died yesterday morning. I sat up with him, with another of the Corps. * * * * * He knew every body by name that came to see him, but in other respects seemed unconscious, and talked in Latin and in Greek. Two or three times he looked at me, and said, '*I wish I was home!*' * * * * We shall miss him very much, he was so kind and social, and was not too proud to come into our tents, and talk and joke with a private soldier."

These are sad, but gratifying and consoling words. Poor boy; I grieved sorely that I could not reach his dying bed, but a father's helping hand, or a mother's tenderest care could have availed nothing then, and it is pleasant to remember, and deeply grateful am I to record the fact, that kind hearts and gentle hands did all for him that lay within the compass of human power. His mind, in its wanderings, recalled the scenes and the companions of his College life, and rested last on his dear home so far away, so hopelessly distant from him, where hearts were then palpitating in the first great agony of their recently awakened fears.

In his classical reminiscences at such an hour, perhaps the Cheronean Epitaph, on which he had exercised his poetic skill, came floating dimly over the broken waves of memory, and I can easily fancy him recalling and murmuring, with a slight change, the Horatian plaint:

"Linquenda tellus, et domus, et placens
Soror; neque harum, quas colis, arborum,
Te preter invisas cupressos,
Ulla brevem dominum sequetur." *

And thus with tender thoughts of his earthly home, where anxious hearts were longing to receive him, and others still, I trust, of that other and better home, where sainted spirits were waiting to welcome him, his soul went gently forth, not "into the great darkness," but may we not devoutly hope, into the clear and blessed sunlight of his God, that God that keepeth covenant and remembereth mercy unto a thousand generations.

* The version of Sir PHILIP FRANCIS, with some little latitude of interpretation, conveys substantially the sense of the original. With a slight modification, to make the adaptation more specific, it is subjoined:

"My loving sister must be left,
And I of country, home bereft,
Must to the shades descend;
The cypress only, mournful tree,
Of all my much-loved groves shall me
Their short-lived lord attend."

Of all this, we in that far-off home could then know nothing. We had heard indeed, in the early hours of the Sabbath morning, that a great battle had been fought on the preceding day, attended, as was said, by some measure of success to the Union arms, but no details were given, and we went calmly to the house of the Lord, and committed, as was our wont, all our anxieties to Him. When Monday, the fifteenth, had passed, and no special intelligence of the Twenty-Sixth was received, save a statement of the wounding of the Lieutenant Colonel, and the loss of many men, we became re-assured, and not until nearly the hour of ten at night, as we sat quietly conversing together, did the first telegraphic dispatch, from a thoughtful friend at Washington, give us a premonition of what, in the early hours of the ensuing morning, was more than confirmed, by another dispatch, announcing the wound, the amputation, and the peril of the sufferer.

I draw a vail over all that then followed; nor need I linger on the third and the most sad and trying journey I immediately made to Washington, accompanied by my friend, and the faithful, devoted friend of my son, Dr. Douglass, to reach, if possible, his side, and minister to him, if it might be, in his dying moments. The effort was vain and fruitless. He was beyond all mortal aid even before we left home, although it was not until I reached Alexandria that the whole truth broke suddenly and fearfully upon me. I have no heart to recall those scenes, save as they are recorded in the letter which on the evening of the day in which I passed through them, I addressed to his mother. I give the details to my friends, as I did to her, by now publishing most of the letter which otherwise few of them would ever see. There are many expressions in it that under ordinary circumstances would not be exposed to the public eye, and that even my friends must kindly and charitably interpret. They were wrung from me by great anguish of heart, struggling with a feeling of high satisfaction that "my boy had done his duty," and died where he preferred to be found, and where I would have chosen to have him, in the van of battle waged for the defense of civilization, humanity and freedom.

WASHINGTON, Dec. 17, 1862, 8 P. M.

* * * * What sad, sad words the telegraph will convey to you to-morrow. It is indeed "all over,—dear WILLIE *has gone home.*" I wrote you as encouragingly as possible this morning, and sent you a

brief dispatch, announcing that our arrangements were all made to go down to the army to-morrow. I shall now try to write as calmly and collectedly as possible of the scenes of this day, and all I now know of the fate of him we so loved.

As we could not leave the city to-day on our projected trip, it occurred to me that I had better take this time to run down to Alexandria, see the Masseys, and tell them of my melancholy errand. I desired also to revisit the spots hallowed to me by the memories of last September, and I feared, if I should find WILLIE gone, I could not trust my poor coward heart so soon to renew these recollections. At three o'clock I went down the river. With eyes swimming in tears, (and yet they were not sad tears,) I looked out on each point we had so often passed together, and his image was there by my side all the while. I walked up the main street, stopped a moment before the door of the shop where I got his crutches made—he will never need them more—and turned into the well-remembered street where is still the hospital. There stood the very bench on which the dear boy sat last September, when with a glad cry we rushed into each other's arms. Oh how freshly the scene came up before me. I passed into the hospital, saw first of all the nurse that was so kind to him, and she wept to hear of his sad wound, and my fears, and expressed a warm hope that he might if possible be brought there again for her to tend and care for. I went up stairs. I stood beside the very cot on which he lay, and from which I took him home, to spend with us those forty happy days we shall remember while memory of any thing remains to us.

I then rang at the door of Mr. Massey, and found one daughter alone at home, to whom I made known my errand, Mr. and Mrs. Massey having gone to Washington. Not expecting to be able to see them, I was about leaving, when Miss M. suddenly saw her father passing the house alone up street. She threw up the window, and pointing to me as I stood before it, beckoned him over. He came across, and I took his hand, saying I had come on a melancholy journey, but hoped still to see my son once more. "*His body is here,*" said he. Oh, how sharp a pang went through my soul, but I commanded myself till Mrs. Massey came. * * * * What a Providence it was that guided my feet there, and has brought me all the way through. You will not weary of these details, and it soothes and assuages the aching sense about my heart, to dwell on them.

And now let me tell you how all this came about. Mr. and Mrs. Massey had returned from Washington in the four o'clock boat. As they landed on the wharf, a tug boat was there, discharging some freight preparatory to going up to Washington, and they heard a soldier use the words, "Adjutant BACON's body." Immediately he stopped to inquire, and found young Millstead with our dear boy's remains, which he had taken charge of and brought all the way, designing to go to Washington, hunt me up, believing that I should be here, and if not, to have the body embalmed and sent home. Mr. M. at once took charge of them, and when passing the house was on his way to the embalmer's. The dear remains had actually passed by the house while I was sitting there! I desired at once to see them, but Mr. M. dissuaded me, saying they would be perfect in the morning, and it was necessary to commence the process at once ; and to-morrow early I shall see his much-loved face. How shall I contain myself? Oh, *how good is*

God ;—what mercy is mingled in this bitter cup. The body had actually been buried in Millstead's absence, but on his return from Aquia Creek, whither he went to send me the message we got on Tuesday morning, he at once had it exhumed, placed in a box, and brought it here for embalming.*

Mr. M. says he is natural, his face was not marred nor distorted. I hope, I believe, I shall bring him to his home : we shall all see his dear dead face here—may we not hope we shall see it radiant in glory ? We shall lay him in the ground our feet will often visit, and when our pilgrimage is done, kind hands will lay us down beside him, "the clods of the valley will be sweet to us," yea sweeter far because we shall slumber beside his precious dust.

I have much to tell you of his fearless bearing in that dreadful, purposeless, and worse than *needless* battle—of the mortal wound, as it truly was before the amputation, which took place but a few hours after he received the fatal stroke—how well he bore it, but how hopeless it was from the very first, and how he began to sink, and gently, as I understand, and at last unconsciously passed away at three or four o'clock *on Tuesday morning,* the hour we were keeping our sad vigils at home, and vainly striving to hope against hope. He had a presentiment before entering the field that it was to be his last battle, and freely expressed it to his young friend, and to others. I doubt not he had the military judgment to see that to hurl infantry against a fortified position overlooking the whole field, with stone walls and earth embankments, bristling with artillery and manned by one hundred thousand men, was to devote

* See note C.

myriads to inevitable destruction. He expressed the belief that it would be fatal to him, but in view of it gave himself to the shock of battle without a thought of faltering or failing in his whole duty. "No braver man," says young Millstead, "ever was, or will be in that regiment." It was horribly depleted, not more than sixty men now answering the roll call. Of the officers, WILLIE lost his life, Lieutenant Colonel Jennings, and Captains Palmer and Shirley, Lieutenants Halstead and our friend Smith, and many more are wounded, but none it is thought seriously.

And so the costly sacrifice the country called for from us is made, but alas! what a price to pay! Not to be mourned over, if a great and happy result had been achieved, but doubly distressing when to private bereavement is to be added national disaster, and the crushing out for the time of the hopes of better fortune we had begun to entertain. But I must not, and I will not, complain. Our lot is not a solitary one. Fathers' and mothers' hearts are rent and bleeding all through the land, and we must be content, for the great cause and the mighty stake the country is playing for, to "stand in our lot," and see, if need be, our household gods shivered around us.

There are many other things you and I will wish to know, but we can not now. What were the exercises of his mind, and what messages he left, and what hopes and desires he expressed. Of these young Millstead knows nothing, for he was with him only at short intervals, but he tells me Dr. Bristol, his good Chaplain, whom he truly respected and loved, was with him, he thinks, nearly all the time, and if so, he must, if reason and consciousness remained, have had conversations more or less with him, and I am sure you will soon have a letter from Dr. B. with some details. I can not persuade myself we shall be deprived of this satisfaction. God has been so good to us in so many of the circumstances of dear WILLIE's life and death, that I feel it not presumption to hope that here also we shall be remembered. I deeply regret that I can not see Dr. B., but situated as the army is, he probably can not leave, and at present I can not go to him. If I could have got to our child, and spoken loving and encouraging words to him, and held his dear hand in mine, and received his last breath: but it was not so to be. I trust he breathed his soul out sweetly to a dearer friend, who loved him infinitely more than I, deep and intense as was and is the love I bore, and still bear to him.

I must bring this to an end, much as it comforts while it saddens me, to talk thus with you of our dear and only son. Like the valiant and true-hearted, "he never tasted death but once," and manly souls and gentler natures will honor and cherish his memory.

* * * * *

The tender and considerate thoughtfulness of Mr. Massey, to whom and to whose family I am under countless obligations, had anticipated all my wishes in respect to the remains; and carefully embalmed, and arrayed for the sepulchre in martial habiliments, his hardships all over, and his warfare ended, with a countenance serene and peaceful, but deeply earnest, "like a warrior taking his rest," he was brought to his home, and on the twenty-fourth of December his funeral obsequies took place in the First Presbyterian Church. That large edifice was crowded to overflowing with a most attentive and sympathizing audience, and the exercises, participated in by President Fisher, of Hamilton College, under whose kind and paternal eye my son had passed the two years of his student life, and by Rev. Dr. Fowler, and Rev. Charles E. Knox, were of the deepest interest and impressiveness. The funeral discourse, by President Fisher, I slightly abbreviate; retaining in full those eloquent, inspiring and feeling utterances that will fall, I am persuaded, on many hearts besides those to which they were mainly addressed, with an elevating, a consoling and a healing power. The text was taken from

John 13 : 7. "WHAT I DO, THOU KNOWEST NOT NOW, BUT THOU SHALT KNOW HEREAFTER."

In the introduction, allusion was made to the grounds and sources of our ignorance of the Divine purposes, arising as it does in part from the limitation of our faculties, and in part from the peculiar constitution of God's kingdom, the way in which he is bringing his sons to glory, and after inculcating the necessity of exercising implicit trust in the power and wisdom and goodness that would be ultimately vindicated, as those purposes should be unfolded and evolved; and making an application of the subject to the occasion, he proceeded thus:

Here, to-day, in the presence of death, where the form of one familiar to you all from childhood, of one reared in all the refined intelligence of a Christian household, the only son, around whom clustered the fondest hopes, the deepest affections, destined, as we fondly anticipated, to bear down the name of his honored sire and grandsire into the future, lies before you, cold and mute, we hear a voice, saying to these stricken hearts, "What I do ye know not now, ye shall know hereafter." I hardly dare trust myself to speak of him as my feelings dictate. Yet it is most fit that those who have fallen for us, whose lives are the costly sacrifice which patriotism offers on the altar of our country, should receive from us the tribute of that affectionate and honored remembrance their heroic devotion demands. We will enshrine them in our grateful memories; we will teach the coming generation to honor their deeds and emulate their lofty patriotism; we will garner their names as they represent the costly jewels we gave to maintain our freedom from the deadly assault of the oppressor.

When, twenty months ago, the conspirators against the free civilization and humanity represented in our National Government, turned their stolen cannon against the feeble, starving garrison in Fort Sumpter, and the sound of those cannon thrilled through the heart and awakened the slumbering patriotism of millions, Adjutant BACON was in yonder halls, successfully preparing for the work of life. He was but a boy, slight in form, impulsive in spirit, with a high sense of honor, always truthful, generous in disposition, fond of the excitements of youth, thinking only that long years must intervene before he could take his place and assume the responsibilities of a man among men. The roar of that fearful assault developed at once another—a manly, a heroic nature. The insult to humanity, the terrible danger that menaced the Government and the institutions of his country, fired his hereditary patriotism, kindled his youthful enthusiasm, absorbed his thoughts, quickened into life the purpose to devote himself to his country. The boy is a boy no longer. At a bound he sprang into the purposes, the responsibilities, the steadiness and the maturity of the man.

One thing alone held in check his patriotic purpose. There were those to whom he owed his being; who had watched over him with parental care; in whose heart of hearts he was shrined as an only son; to whom he had been a dutiful and loving child; would they consent to the costly sacrifice, would they peril all their hopes for him, as yet a stranger to the love of Jesus? He knew, in part, their true patriotism; he knew more fully the love that rested in sunlight on himself. Could that love surrender to his country the child of so many hopes? With devout prayer for guidance to Him who never had failed them in the hour of need, the sacrifice is made. They had given him to God in childhood; they were educating him to be a blessing to his race and country; and now that the interests of humanity, the dearest interests of their country were in peril, they committed him afresh to God and gave him to his country. Sublime patriotism! Sublime Christian devotion! that, with all the perilous paths he was to tread before them, could calmly, confidently leave him with his God, and lay him on the altar of his country! The decision is made: and among the first enrolled in the first company of the first regiment that went from this city, to illustrate our patriotism in resistance to treason, stands the name of WILLIAM KIRKLAND BACON. He is at first only a private; but in a few weeks he attained a position which his talents and attainments qualified him to fill—the Adjutancy of the Twenty-Sixth Regiment. By patient study, his quick intelligence soon made him master of his position—wasting no time in frivolous pleasures, devoting himself with manly earnestness to his work, treading the temptations to vice, which have despoiled so many of our officers of their crown, beneath his feet, he soon gained an enviable and honorable prominence in his regiment. How he grew in the respect and affection of both officers and privates;

how his manly and pure character developed itself day by day; how he proved himself one to be depended upon, alike in the camp and in the field, ye who were his fellow soldiers can testify, as his associates in office have often testified. It was my great pleasure to visit him in camp at Fort Lyon, some nine months ago, and I know that this testimony is true. Subsequent events deepened this respect, and installed him in the hearts of his regiment as a brave—a heroic, as well as a wise and faithful soldier. Through all the marches and countermarches of that long summer campaign, how nobly did he bear himself! Prompt in action, fearless in presence of danger, asking no man to go where he was unwilling to lead, enduring hardships under which ripe manhood sank, the same calm, earnest soul, in the shock of battle and the quiet of the camp. What a striking scene was that, when in the second great conflict on the bloody soil of Manassas, the regiment had been disordered by the flight of another regiment rushing through them, bearing away the superior officers, this boy-soldier dismounted from his wounded and unmanageable horse, took the command, and waving his sword, exhorted the men, "for the sake of God and their country, not to disgrace themselves," and then led them on to battle! Who would not follow where such a young hero led? Who could be a coward where that youthful voice exhorted to duty? And who of all that regiment, now alas! so broken, that would not have carried him in their arms and hearts to victory?

Wounded in that terrible conflict, the young hero returns for a few days to recruit beneath the parental roof. How precious, how comforting were those golden days to those now bowed and stricken hearts, they only know! Changed he was—greatly changed from the boy who left them eighteen months before. The current of his affections seemed to run deeper and fuller; his impulsive nature was steadier and stronger; he spoke but little, and then with great modesty, of what he had done; but the whole tone of his character inspired in their hearts the hope that his affections were setting themselves on One who is alone able to save. The hours, the days flew swiftly by. Before his wound was fully healed, the impulse of duty bade him depart. His brave compatriots were in the field, why should he linger here? The romance of war had lost its attractions; he knew too well its stern, often sad and fearful character; he knew that he was going to danger, perhaps to death. He did not hesitate. The sense of duty, the impulse of patriotism, the voice of his country urged him on. When his honored father, as he took leave of him for the last time, said, "Good-by! trust in the Lord and do your whole duty," with characteristic modesty he replied, "Depend upon it, father, I will try." These were the parting words. We hasten to the end. Immediately joining his regiment, he at once resumed his position and marched to Fredericksburg. The dispositions are all made for the fearful conflict. On the morning of that eventful day, he expressed to his Lieutenant Colonel his conviction that he would fall. The Colonel rallied him a little, and told him he was homesick. He answered, "Colonel, no man on earth has a dearer home than I have, but if a wish could place me there now, I would not go. My place is here, and here I remain." Strange and mysterious is the fact that God so often permits the shadow of death to be thrown upon us, that we may prepare ourselves for his coming! In this calm, heroic spirit, leaning as we have reason to believe on an arm unseen by the eye of sense, he moved forward with his regiment. The Twenty-Sixth stood like a wall of iron amidst the storm of death hurtling its fiery missiles through its ranks. The scene for him is over. The messenger sought him and found him. He lingers for three days and then his young spirit ascended to his God. Dear WILLIE, thou art gone—gone from us forever. We shall counsel and instruct thee no more, for another teacher infinitely wise and good is now leading thee up the heights of knowledge, and in a moment thou hast learnt more than men on earth can ever know.

To us Christians, the deepest interest gathers about the future of the immortal spirit. Patriotism is not religion, although Christianity produces the loftiest and purest patriotism. Must we then close this short record of this young life here, and leave him with his God? I can not thus, in justice to him, refuse to express the convictions that have formed themselves in my mind. I would indeed that his faithful Chaplain, that true man of God, whom he loved as a father, were here in my place; gladly would I be the listener to his eloquent words, rather than address to you my own imperfect utterances. I believe that God is a covenant keeping God, that he hears and answers prayer, and that often, by ways to us strange and mysterious, he leads the child of prayer into the fold. Not in vain for so many years was this dear youth borne in the arms of prayer and nourished by Christian counsel. "What I do thou knowest not now, but thou shalt know hereafter." Strange it is to us that the discipline of the camp and the battle-field, should be the path along which God would lead him to himself.

Yet it is in this way his sovereignty has answered prayer. The vices which overmastered others, wakened to life in him those principles which parental love had planted there. He went to the word of God for counsel; he tried not only to do his duty to his country but to his God; with prayer for divine protection he prepared himself for battle. Confiding in One almighty to save, he gave himself a sacrifice on that last fatal field. I can not state to you the many indications that have wrought in those who loved him most tenderly and knew him most fully, the conviction that their dear child is passed into the heavens. Yes! my dear friends, that God who gave you courage to offer this great sacrifice, has given you likewise the sustaining conviction, that through this stern discipline your beloved has passed into that better life. Not in vain has been your agony! Not in vain have been your humble pleadings at the throne of grace. Beyond the stars, in that bright world where separations are unknown, you will meet again. There you will recognize with joy unspeakable all the way in which your Redeemer has led you, and parents, sisters, brother, stand and praise before the throne.

I turn from you, who to-day share the deep sympathies of this assembly in your affliction, to others here present.

Soldiers of the Twenty-Sixth and Fourteenth, you have come to see a beloved comrade borne to his last earthly home. His last battle has been fought: no drum beat will ever again rouse him from his slumbers; no shrill bugle call him to the field. He has gone where war is unknown; where the peace of God fills the heart, and henceforth he lives to die no more. You have borne a noble part in this great struggle; when others hesitated, you rushed to the field. For us you have fought; for us you have braved danger and endured hardship. A grateful country will not forget you. When peace shall again lift her milk-white standard over the proud dome of our Capitol, and the flag you have defended shall again wave in triumph over a united and free country, then will it be your pride and glory, the proud inheritance of your children, that you gave yourselves to that country in her hour of need.

But, soldiers, there is one battle greater than this you are to fight, one wreath of victory of infinitely greater value you are to win and wear. There is a a fight of faith within your own hearts, to be fought; there is a crown of righteousness, unfading and eternal, to be won. God help you in this great conflict; Jesus, the Captain of Salvation, make you victors over yourselves, and lead you on to glory. Then will all the glory of these earthly conflicts grow dim before the grandeur and the brightness of your last and greatest victory.

And here to-day are young men, and men in their early prime, hardy, vigorous, able to do and suffer for God and your country. You weep to-day with these bereaved ones over their early-lost. But why is that body lifeless and mute? Why is it that youth, just passing out of boyhood, must wage this fearful warfare, while the mature and the strong are busy about their usual avocations? Our country is bleeding at every pore; the cries of distressed patriotism pierce every ear and enter every heart. Is there one here that does not love his country? Let him shed no tear over that coffin; let him not look on that pale, pleading countenance. But if to-day, you feel that the blood which courses through your veins;

the breath that heaves your lungs; the intelligence that lights up your eyes; the limbs strong for labor, all—all belong to the country that has nourished you on her bosom and shed upon you the influences that have made you what you are, and exalted you among the nations; then, while first of all, as Christ's minister, I exhort you to prepare to meet your God in peace, I would not, I can not forbear to remind you, that it is for you, as your next highest and most imperative duty, to stand by that country, to give her your prayers, and as she calls, fear not to give yourselves a living sacrifice for her salvation. That coffin, those mute lips, appeal to all your manhood, to all your patriotism, to follow where this our young hero so nobly led.

Fellow-citizens, this is no idle pageant, this no ordinary death, these no common funeral solemnities. The lessons of this hour reach far into the future, and will mould the destinies of unborn generations. When we are gathered to the house appointed for all living, this sacrifice, and those kindred to it, which now shroud so many families in sackcloth, will bear precious fruit. The millions who are yet to people this vast continent, who are here to rejoice in the freedom of the Gospel, who are to spread that Gospel in all its light and freedom through the world, will thrill at the mention of their names, will bless God for the spirit that nerved them for the sacrifice, and that baptism of blood through which he secured for them so priceless an inheritance. Let us anticipate that day; let us prove ourselves worthy of such memories; let us consecrate ourselves, body and soul, to him who suffered for us, and lifting high the standard of a pure Christianity, count no sacrifice too great, no achievement too difficult, that is to exalt our fallen humanity and prepare the pathway for the Prince of Peace. Then at length, when the shadow of the last hour shall fall upon us, looking forward to the great resurrection, we may exclaim: "I have fought a good fight, I have finished my course, I have kept the faith; henceforth there is laid up for me a crown of righteousness, which the Lord, the righteous judge, will give me in that day."

At the close of the service, youthful and loyal hands—for no others were worthy to bear the precious remains—took up the bier of the young soldier, and thus was he borne to the pleasant Cemetery, where he will rest with his fathers until the morning that a trump above the clangor of battle or the shouts of contending armies, shall call the sleeping dead to judgment.

Manifold and exceedingly consoling were the public and private testimonials we received of the estimation in which our son was held, and they all have a place among our household treasures. Those from his young college companions, and from the privates of the Twenty-Sixth, were most touching and gratifying; testifying, as they all did, to his genial kindness of heart and the manly intrepidity of his nature. I need not reproduce them here; but among the private communications made to his parents, there are a few to which a more specific though brief allusion may properly be made. In a letter written to us from the camp, after his death, by the Chaplain, Dr. Bristol, he says: "WILLIE was a noble boy. I loved him almost as I would a son. He was brave and generous. He was manly above his years—a HERO—what more can I say of the brave, the lamented dead; only that I hope the prayers of the home-altar were answered upon his soul. He had his serious hours, and always talked with me freely and candidly on the great subject of religion."

Capt. George Arrowsmith, (now Lieutenant Colonel of the 157th New York Volunteers,) with whom he had an association of great intimacy, says: "It is difficult for me to realize that the warmest friendship I have formed since I have been in the army is thus severed. Yet that which had been a source of pleasure is now the source of pride, and sorrow for him we have lost has some mitigation in our admiration for the departed hero."

Dr. Abraham L. Cox, in a letter subsequent to the one which will be found in the Appendix, reiterates, in the warmest manner, his own estimate of the chivalrous bearing and manly fortitude of my son, and gives a beautiful and affecting illustration of the soldierly pride he felt at the moment of his own utter prostration, in the fact that his regiment had so nobly breasted the shock of battle. He kindly adds: "The first whisper of ill-feeling or of censure against Adjutant BACON is yet to be made. Universally admired, he had no enemies. In the field I have heard from the General his satisfaction with his military promptitude and accuracy. Gen. Tower's praise is what every military man who knows him regards as the highest plaudit."

The allusion here is to Brig. Gen. Z. B. Tower, who was in command of the brigade at Manassas, and there received a grievous wound, from which he has not yet recovered. The manner in which he led the brigade on that occasion excited the warmest admiration of my son, and although he never made any personal application for such a post, I remember his often expressing a strong wish that he could be in some way attached to his military staff. It is a great gratification to his friends to learn, as they now do from a letter addressed to me by Gen. Tower, that had circumstances permitted it, such a position would have been tendered him. I know very well how easy it is to say kind things of the dead, and how strong the inducement to soothe the sensibilities and minister perhaps to the undue pride of a father's heart. I shall frankly expose myself to this impeachment, since I can not resist the temptation to make a somewhat copious extract from this communication of Gen. Tower: "My short acquaintance," he says, "with Adjutant BACON prepossessed me greatly in his favor. I could not but notice his manly and soldierly bearing, and his promptitude and efficiency in performing his duties. I should have offered him a position on my personal and military staff, had I returned to the brigade after the battle of August thirtieth. It is a pleasing duty to inform you on reliable authority, that in this battle your son was distinguished for gallant services at the head of his regiment, until his wound forced him from the field. At Fredericksburgh he was conspicuous for manly bravery and cool determination, an example to his soldiers, till he fell mortally wounded on that never to be forgotten battle-field. It is a noble grief to drop the tear of sorrow on his grave. His brilliant military career seems to be all that parental pride could hope for, save that it was too quickly ended. But it will live in the memory of his friends and acquaintances, and all those who may learn his history."

Laus est, a laudato viro, laudari.

Rev. Charles E. Knox, who was pastor for two years of the Church where his family and himself were worshipers and attendants, wrote us a most tender, cheering and consoling letter, from which I make the following extract: "What nobler end could there have been to his life, what higher purpose could he have accomplished, even in a life prolonged to twice or thrice its length? Could we have made a better life-plan, if we had been permitted to try, than God has now revealed that He had made for him; one which would have been more honorable to him, more noble in its support of the highest and best principles, and more helpful to the Kingdom of our Saviour. How blessed it is to be permitted to think that God was preparing him by the stern discipline of war for his everlasting peace; and what a privilege was his life, to stand battling to the death for the right, at the point where all the great principles of justice, truth, freedom and religion converge."

His religious character, so far as it had outward manifestation, must be judged of in part by the glimpses afforded by his correspondence, and was more fully developed to us by communications more private and confidential still; so that the friends that knew him best, have the most hope and comfort in his death. We knew from his own lips that before he went into the battle of Manassas, he devoutly commended himself to God, and we can not doubt that in the last and closing scene, with its solemn premonitions before him, he in like manner, and with a deeper consciousness of its necessity, put soul and body into the keeping of his Saviour. I add one little circumstance here, which will, I think, greatly interest his friends. Among the mementos he took with him, and which accompanied him in all his wanderings, and were returned to us after his death, were a number of books, and among them a pocket Bible, the gift of a young friend, accompanied by her photograph, and a miniature edition of the Book of Psalms. I had also, when he first left home, given him my photograph on a card, upon the back of which I had written the sentiment popularly ascribed to Cromwell: "Put your trust in the Lord, and keep your powder dry." On opening these two books after they reached us, we found the first photograph inserted in the Bible at the nineteenth and twentieth Psalms, and the other in the same place precisely in the Book of Psalms. It is possible this may have been a casual and undesigned location, but the coincidence is certainly remarkable, and I am persuaded it was not without a thought and purpose. Is it unreasonable to suppose that in the twelfth, thirteenth and fourteenth verses of the nineteenth Psalm, and in the seventh verse of the twentieth Psalm, he found something apposite to his own condition and wants, and a tower of strength upon which he felt both desire and encouragement to lean?

I can not refrain from adding one tribute to his memory, which coming from the quarter it did, and accompanied by a most appropriate gift of a cross of immortelles for the soldier's breast, deeply affected us. It will be found in the appended note.*

My task is done. The work has insensibly grown upon my hands, and has been protracted beyond my original design. It has been executed in much infirmity, and with many distractions of mind, amid swelling tides of grief, mitigated and

* See note D.

assuaged indeed by help Divinely given, alternating with proud and consoling recollections of him who was "my joy and my crown," and a strong hope that his example might stimulate others in like manner to devote themselves to the good and great cause, the cause that by the blessing of God shall ultimately prevail, shall finally triumph. It is this spirit of consecration that can alone save our dear country in this the crucial hour of its destiny. I count no sacrifice too great or costly to secure this noble end; and in this faith and hope of final success I firmly abide. I shall never surrender it, until I am prepared to abandon my trust in truth, in righteousness and in freedom, and above all, in God, the author and defender of them all. I shall utter no reproach, but I profoundly pity those who have no sympathy with this mighty effort to roll back the flood of crime and barbarism that threaten to engulf us, and have no personal stake in the great issue; and on the other hand, I have nothing but words of earnest encouragement and hearty cheer to those who stand by the country and "rally on the flag" of the free.

What follows is the contribution of another hand; of one that knew WILLIE as well, and loved him as devotedly as any of the circle by which he was surrounded. I will not appropriate this to myself, nor can I suppress it, containing as it does the impression, perhaps exaggerated as to some it may seem, but to others truthful and just, of a young but glorious life.

Here we close this brief record, knowing that it is not the history of one alone, but of hundreds of young lives as blameless and precious as the one we commemorate, and who, with all their wealth of courage and patriotism, of hope and promise, have been laid upon the altar of their country, seemingly as yet an unaccepted sacrifice.

We would not recall the past. The qualities which so much endeared him to us, were the very ones which led him to danger and to death. Cold calculation, selfish indolence, hesitation, cowardice, would have saved him, but we would not buy even that dear life back again, on terms like these; and his unstained memory is a thousand times more precious to us than his actual presence could be, if shorn of those treasures of mind and heart which made him the pride and joy of our household. Yet the crushing out of so many fond hopes, the desolation of a once happy home, are wounds which time can not heal; and loving hearts will still sometimes involuntarily turn from the past to dwell upon the possible future, and all that he might have been had it been the will of Heaven to spare him to us yet a little longer. Slain upon the threshold of a noble manhood, he will never return to fulfill the fair promises of his youth. With a character only partially developed, but growing daily in strength and beauty, life for him was full of bright anticipations of usefulness and happiness. His genial, generous and affectionate nature, drew around him kind and warm friends, wherever he went, and among all classes. True hearted and sincere, he rarely lost a regard once won. The moral strength which he had acquired in his successful struggle with the temptations of college and camp life, at an age when the powers of resistance are weakest, gave us confidence to believe that having borne unflinchingly those severe tests, under which so many fail, he would maintain his integrity to the end. The pride of his Puritan blood, unlike that which springs from a less worthy source, showed itself in no haughty assumption or boastful arrogance, but simply wrought in him a manly independence, subdued with a graceful modesty, a high sense of honor, a scorn of every form of meanness, a firm fidelity to duty, an intelligent patriotism, an unshaken resolution to maintain to the last a cause which he had once conscientiously espoused — qualities which assured to him, if not a brilliant, yet what is better, an honorable career. He was by nature exceedingly generous, illustrations of which his friends will readily recall, without a trace of a calculating or money-making spirit, and his plans of benevolence were always formed on the most liberal scale, yet he had already developed a capacity for business, of which in his earlier years he gave no intimation. His neatly kept accounts, his carefully arranged letters and papers, his promptness in the performance of every duty, his punctuality in the payment of debts, all testify to the fact that he possessed the plain, practical virtues of justice and honesty, as well as that impulsive generosity which would lead him to share his last dollar with a friend in distress. The qualities which gave him so fair a reputation in the army, admirably fitted him to serve his country in the character of a good and peaceable citizen; but his duties as a citizen he was never destined to fulfill, and even his military career was too brief to permit more than a partial development of that ability he was thought to possess. He was a true soldier. Honor and loyalty reigned in his heart and guided his life. Of his courage it is unnecessary to speak: to souls like his, capable of a high purpose and a deep enthusiasm, the presence of danger is always an inspiration. His standard of drill and discipline was very high, yet his genial manner, his kind smile and pleasant words, his unselfish interest in the comfort and welfare of the men, made him one of the most popular officers in the regiment. With a talent for command, he united a deep sense of the duty of subordination. He seemed too much absorbed in his own duties to find time for very profound speculation on the merits of different commanders, —to criticise one officer, or cultivate a blind devotion for another. He fought wholly for his country, never for an individual. No degree of distrust of one general, or of confidence in another, could affect his resolution to fight as long and as well as he knew how, no matter who gave the orders.

Though he bore up steadily and manfully under hardship and disaster, his proud and sensitive spirit felt keenly at times the mortification of defeat. Yet he was not discouraged. Reverses, instead of disheartening him, seemed only to kindle an intenser indignation, and develop a more determined spirit of opposition to the enemies of his country. "The next time," said he, "we will fight as every man must fight if we ever expect to succeed in this war. The Twenty-Sixth shall stand until every man is shot down, rather than retreat an inch. Whatever may happen to the rest of the army, our regiment shall not be beaten again." Faithfully did the noble Twenty-Sixth fulfill the prophecy at Fredericksburgh.

It matters little now, yet as we look back upon the history of the last eighteen months, there is something inexpressibly sad and touching in the thought that he, in common with the rest of our brave but unfortunate army, was called upon to endure so much of the hardship, toil and trial of a soldier's life, with so few of its compensations. To one tenderly cherished, as he was, with all his reasonable wants gratified, and his desires almost anticipated, those trials and hardships, in the main so cheerfully borne, will not be counted among the least of the sacrifices he was called upon to make. Hunger, cold, heat, fatigue, long, weary marches, ending in disappointment or disaster; the humiliation of defeat, and at last, wounds, suffering and death, were all his portion, yet he never knew the reward of the brave and faithful soldier; and even in his dying hour he was denied the joy of victory, or the proud thought that by his sacrifice he had aided to "win the battle for the free."

Yet in the bitterness of our sorrow let us not forget to acknowledge, with humble and grateful hearts, the great goodness and mercy of God. Let us thank Him that He gave to one whom we dearly loved, so noble a work to do on earth, and that He enabled him to do it so faithfully and so well; that if die he must at this time, he was permitted to die upon the battle-field, not in an unholy warfare or an unjust cause, not coldly turning away from the call of his country, or secretly sympathizing with her foes, but in the way of his duty and in the defense of the right;—that he has left behind him so stainless a name, and so sweet and precious a memory; that having fulfilled his earthly mission, and yielded up his young life upon the sacred shrine of freedom and humanity, he has gone to join the noble army of martyrs who surround the throne with songs of victory, there to share in the triumphs of his Lord and Saviour, and to dwell in the light of His glory forever.

APPENDIX.

Note A.

BY PROFESSOR EDWARD NORTH, OF HAMILTON COLLEGE.

As a student in Hamilton College, Adjutant Bacon showed a fine appreciation of the beautiful in art and letters, with a skill beyond his years in the rhythmical use of words. What he could do with his ready pen, was known only to a few. In his early death, his more intimate friends mourn the untimely loss of a promising poet, as well as an accurate and elegant scholar. His reading of Homer and Horace was not done perfunctorily, but with an evident perception and relish of that which gives them pre-eminence as classical authors.

In the fall of 1860, he read the Oration of Demosthenes, *De Corona.* Near the close of this master-piece of eloquence, Demosthenes recites the inscription from a costly monument erected by the Athenians in honor of their countrymen who fell at Cheronea. It was proposed to the Sophomores, as a voluntary exercise, to translate this inscription into English verse.

While others undertook the task in iambics, Adjutant Bacon rendered the epitaph into graceful dactyls, thus closely imitating the original Greek, and showing that he was competent to manage the most difficult rhythm in our language. Of course, a literal translation could not be made, under the conditions proposed. If the sentiment and spirit of the Greek were put into appropriate verse, the effort would be praiseworthy.

Leland's translation of this epitaph, that runs through twenty iambic lines, is considered an elaborate failure. Thomas Campbell's version, in ten compact and vigorous lines, was contributed, by special request, to Lord Brougham's edition of the *De Corona*.

For the convenience of any who may wish to compare the two, we copy, first, the original Greek, and then Adjutant BACON's rendering:

'ΕΠΙΓΡΑΜΜΑ.

Οἵδε πάτρας ἕνεκα σφετέρας εἰς δῆριν ἔθεντο
Ὅπλα, καὶ ἀντιπάλων ὕβριν ἀπεσκέδασαν.
Μαρνάμενοι δ' ἀρετῆς καὶ δείματος οὐκ ἐσάωσαν.
Ψυχάς, ἀλλ' Ἀΐδην κοινὸν ἔθεντο βράβην,
Οὕνεκεν Ἑλλήνων, ὡς μὴ ζυγὸν αὐχένι θέντες
Δουλοσύνης στυγερὰν ἀμφὶς ἔχωσιν ὕβριν.
Γαῖα δὲ πατρὶς ἔχει κόλποις τῶν πλεῖστα καμόντων
Σώματ', ἐπεὶ θνητοῖς ἐκ Διὸς ἥδε κρίσις.
Μηδὲν ἁμαρτεῖν ἐστὶ θεῶν καὶ πάντα κατορθοῦν
Ἐν βιοτῇ, μοῖραν δ' οὔ τι φυγεῖν ἔπορεν.

TRANSLATION.

These are the heroes who fought for their father-land's weal,
Taking up arms to resist the invader's proud steel.
Bravely they fought, and their souls to grim Pluto they gave,
Cheerfully offering up life, their loved country to save.
Scorning to humble their souls to slavery's force,
Death brought them less to lament than slavery's curse.
Father-land lovingly takes to its sacred breast
Forms that in bloodiest strife found their honored rest.
Never to fail in life's work, falls to none under Heaven:
Jove is the giver of all, and to these death was given.

This College exercise may serve as an illustration of Adjutant BACON's scholarship and intellectual character. Yet we would not have recalled it here, did not the

Cheronean Epitaph, as rendered by him, read to-day like a prophetic adumbration of his own sadly-glorious end. Little did the light-hearted student of 1860 dream, as he toyed with the fascinating perplexities of Attic poetry, that he was preparing a fit epitaph for thousands of brave Union heroes, doomed to be slain in the battles of 1862, himself being one of the number.

Another well-known trait in the character of Adjutant BACON, his unaffected and endearing modesty, is revealed in the record of this voluntary task, which closes with an excerpt from Horace:

"Si quid tamen olim
Scripseris, in Meti descendat judicis auras
Et patris, et nostras, nonumque prematur in annum,
Membranis intus positis."

Spirit of WILLIE, forgive the feeling that submits to the charity of friends what you intended only for the eyes of your teacher!

NOTE B.

HEAD-QUARTERS 2D BRIGADE 2D DIVISION 1ST ARMY CORPS,
LEFT GRAND DIVISION OF THE ARMY OF THE POTOMAC,
Dec. 28th, 1862, (near Fredericksburgh, Virginia.)

MY DEAR HANSON,—Yours of the 23d inst., just received, demands of me what my heart prompted me almost to do unasked,—to say a few words in regard to the excellent and brave boy of Judge Bacon. He was an officer in the Twenty-Sixth Regiment, N. Y. Vols., one of the regiments of my brigade. I was well acquainted with him, and have great satisfaction in being able to express my entire conviction of the worth of character and gentlemanly bearing which always made him a marked man in an army which I may truly say abounds in excellent characters. Always efficient in the performance of duty, he possessed a winning, graceful and universally popular manner towards every one. Pure in morals, and unassuming in manners, he enjoyed an enviable prestige in the army. I saw him in the retreat from the battle of Manassas, wounded, on horseback, but cheerful and modest as usual, and was particular to stop and converse with him, as he had been reported to me to have been fatally wounded.

At the hospital near Fredericksburgh, I was one of the three principal operators, and felt especially for him the solicitude of a friend as well as the anxiety always experienced by us on the arrival of a bad case. His was eminently such. It consisted of a wound of the thigh, in the upper third, with great injury of the bone, which was terribly splintered. Now in the experience of military surgery for the last two centuries, this sort of wound has been fatal in every instance where amputation *is not performed.* The celebrated Guthrie, in his account of the Surgery of the Peninsular war, states the proportion of deaths after primary amputations, (that is, operations performed soon,) at 33 per cent., while that of cases deferred for a day or two, at double that amount. It became a question with us at once what was to be done, and I called my two colleagues to consult with me in his case, as well as Doctor Charles J. Nordquist, the able surgeon, now of the 1st corps of this division, before I would decide on an operation, and determine whether he had not received such a shock from the injury, as to forbid any operation whatever. He was excessively prostrated, but desired amputation. We administered to him the proper restoratives, and after a while had the satisfaction to observe from them the most flattering effects, such as improvement in his pulse, countenance and spirits. When the reaction justified it, we lost no time. The opinion expressed however at the time by Nordquist, was that it was a bad case, and one where life would not probably be saved. I was myself very much disposed to the same opinion. The operation was however his only chance of life, and there was perfect unanimity with the surgeons as to the course of procedure. He was placed under the influence of chloroform which acted most favorably. He was entirely insensible to pain, the stump was dressed and pronounced a perfect operation, as it was a very rapid one. He seemed better, and recovered very much after the amputation, and was nursed by Major Sellers, himself wounded, and by Dr. Walter B. Coventry, an admirable surgeon, who was in general charge of the hospital. He was placed in a fine room, on as good a bed as his father's house could furnish, and watched and nursed incessantly. After every operation I performed, I made it a rule to visit him and attend to his case, and I can assure you this duty was performed by me as a friend, rather than as a mere surgeon. He did not suffer much, complained little if at all, smiled whenever I visited him, but did not react with the vigor I desired. Along side of him, in the same room, was a Captain, who complained more, seemed as much prostrated, but reacted better. I at first thought their cases equally critical, and the result in the two cases only proves the difference in the constitutions of individuals.

Adjutant Bacon preserved after his wound and the operation, the same equal mind which characterized him in health, and his fortitude then was equal to his bravery in action.

It may be remarked that he went into the action with

a presentiment of his being fatally wounded. I received this from one of his fellow officers. How far this feeling may have exerted a depressing tendency I cannot say, but believe that in his case the cause of the fatal result was the first terrible shock to his system.

There are no particular expressions of his that I can recall, as he was more remarkable for his modesty, patience and fortitude, than for a disposition to express to others what he thought or felt.

On the whole, you may assure his friends that his death was glorious in every respect, whether we regard his patriotism towards his country, or his private virtues and the elevation of character manifested in his never uttering a complaint during his confinement, so far as I can testify, and never losing the dignity, serenity and manliness which belonged to him in health.

Col. Peter Lyle, now in command of the brigade, speaks in high terms of Adjutant BACON, and so does every officer in his regiment, and all sincerely lament his loss and sympathize with his bereaved relatives.

Joining in these sentiments myself very cordially, I beg you to present to his father and family the assurance of my own sympathy, and my deep sense of their loss, in which I feel myself in some degree an humble sharer.

Your affectionate uncle,

ABM. L. COX

REV. SAMUEL HANSON COXE.

Note C.

I was quite surprised, and somewhat tried when this fact first came to my knowledge. I had from an early day, in anticipation of the fatal event, made it my earnest request and emphatic direction, that in case of his death, the body of my son should not be committed to the soil of any rebel State, but carefully embalmed and sent home to rest with his fathers. But a letter subsequently received from the Chaplain contained a full and most satisfactory explanation of the whole matter. It appears that on the morning of his death, there was a strong expectation that the batteries of the rebels would be opened and shell the north bank of the river. Orders were therefore at once given to remove the wounded from the hospitals and bury the dead. The Chaplain proposed to carry the body to the rear on his horse, but Dr. Nordquist strongly advised the burial of the remains for the purposes of preservation, and so marking the grave that they could be easily recovered. "Under these circumstances," says Dr. Bristol, "I reluctantly consented to lay him down in his lonely bed. Those who loved him, silently and sadly hollowed out his narrow resting place, and John Geers, George Primmer, William O'Brien and George Bradley, of the Twenty-Sixth, carried him gently out and laid him down to rest. I rudely lettered his name on a board to mark his grave, and thus we left him." It was a kind and thoughtful act, and to it I am indebted for the better preservation of the remains and their safe and speedy recovery.

Note D.

THE YOUTHFUL MARTYR.

The following exquisite lines, the production of a gifted lady of this city, were sent by the author to the parents of the late Adjutant Bacon. At their earnest solicitation, the writer has consented to their publication, that other hearts thus sorely visited, may in like manner be consoled :

Oh, falter not to yield him now
  Brave hearts, that gave your only son ;
But still before the Father bow
  And say in truth, "Thy will be done."

Like faithful Abraham of old,
  Ye offered him in sacrifice,
Which God will in remembrance hold,
  And recompense beyond the skies.

For hath not Christ, the Lamb, been slain
  That they who through obedience grieve,
May at his own right hand again
  Their precious ones in joy receive ?

Thus may your tears submissive flow
  For him whose warfare now is o'er,
Who never more a wound shall know,
  Safe landed on the eternal shore.

The early martyred to the truth,
  To him the martyr's crown is given,
Unbroken peace, immortal youth,
  And palms of victory in Heaven.

ERRATUM.

In the note at the bottom of page 43, instead of "Sir" before the name of Philip Francis, read "Dr."

ADDENDA.

The following account of the presentation of the foregoing "MEMORIAL" to the classmates of Adjutant BACON, communicated to the Utica *Morning Herald* by Prof. Edward North, is published here at the urgent request of the class, communicated to the author, and is intended for distribution almost exclusively among these his College friends and companions.

PROCEEDINGS OF THE SENIOR CLASS.

HAMILTON COLLEGE, June 12, 1863.

TO THE EDITOR OF THE UTICA MORNING HERALD:

The monotony of College life was relieved this afternoon by a touching tribute to the memory of Adjutant BACON, that will not soon be effaced from the memory of those who were present. The final examination of the class of 1863, of which Adjutant BACON was a worthy member, is now in progress. At the opening of the afternoon session, Judge Bacon came before the class, and with a brief address presented each of the classmates of his son with a copy of the "Memorial of Adjutant

BACON," which has just appeared from the press of E. H. Roberts. The presentation was gracefully and feelingly accepted by the Valedictorian of the class, Mr. CHARLES VAN NORDEN, of New York.

The address of Judge Bacon was as follows:

I have long cherished the desire, my young friends, the classmates and companions of my departed son, to meet you in this quiet and unostentatious way. I have wished to look into your faces, and spend a few moments in reviving for a short space at least, our mutual remembrances of one who has so recently passed away from the troubled and tumultuous scenes of earth to the quiet of the grave, and as I am humbly permitted to hope, to the peace and rest of Heaven.

With many, if not with the most of you, he started four years ago upon one stage of life's journey, the goal of which you are just about to reach. The prizes and the honors, and what is better, the solid attainments for which you have worthily striven, are already, or are soon to be yours. He has fallen by the way, not because he was unfit for the race, or a laggard in the arena, but because it pleased God to call him to another service, and give him early the crown of martyrdom in a just and righteous cause.

Your regard, your sympathies, and your prayers I trust went with him, as I know his affections strongly were with you, and one of the happy thoughts that gilded his homeward prospect, when as he hoped he should return from a service honorably and faithfully fulfilled, was that although he might not partake of your honors, he would at least stand by your side on the day of your graduation, and proudly and joyfully say, "These were my classmates."

It may be known to you that I have employed some leisure hours of the past winter, in collecting a few materials and preparing a simple record of his short, but not altogether uneventful life. It has been a sad, and yet I may say upon the whole a pleasing duty, performed indeed in much weakness, and which will I hope receive, what it needs, the charitable judgment of my friends, and the friends of my son.

A copy of this Memorial I desire to, and now propose to place in the hands of each one of his classmates. You will receive it as the gift of one who is united to you not only by the tie of a common brotherhood, but by associations that touch the deepest fountains of feeling within my heart. It is a very brief record, for life with him was compressed and compacted substantially into a few months, but unless I am entirely deceived, even this short life has in it lessons of principle, devotion and sacrifice that young hearts may admire and emulate, and older heads not unprofitably ponder. It contains the substance of all I have been able to gather, or my own personal knowledge and reflection have supplied me with, concerning his acts, and the motives and impulses that prompted them.

You all remember the electric shock that thrilled the land when traitorous hands leveled their deadly missives at the feeble garrison of Sumpter and the good old flag that proudly floated above it. You knew the impulsive, and I may say here I suppose without impeachment, the intrepid character of my son. He felt that stain like a wound, and with scarce a pause for reflection, sprang instinctively to the post of duty and of danger. On the twelfth of April, 1861, rebel guns stolen from the Government, opened upon Fort Sumpter; on the fifteenth the President's proclamation called for seventy-five thousand volunteers; on the nineteenth WILLIE preferred his dutiful request to be one of the number; gained full and free parental consent, and on the morning of the twentieth was enrolled as a private in the Fourteenth Regiment of N. Y. Volunteers. His career from that time to the day when with bowed heads but unmurmuring hearts, we laid him down to his final earthly rest, is told, I hope without exaggeration, in these few pages. You will read them for his sake. You will see that in his closing hours, half unconscious as they were, busy memory recalled the scenes of his College life, and mingled them with his dear home, and those who tenderly cherished him there. If tears shall glisten in your eyes at the perusal, they will not stain your manly cheeks, for of him I may say without arrogance, and of each of you with little liability to misconception,

> "Multis ille bonis flebilis occidit,
> Nulli flebilior, quam tibi."

There is no need, perhaps no propriety, my young friends, that I should speak to you of the personal and social qualities that marked his character. Like all fathers, I can not claim exemption from the blind side, which is inevitable from our position, and of course I am liable to misjudge his motives and over-estimate his conduct. To me however he was ever eminently frank and truthful; the sweetest and most unreserved confidence existed between us; I was one of the sharers of his joys and sorrows, and if ever I had the privilege of looking down into a human soul transparently opened to my gaze, I persuade myself that I possessed it fully in respect to him. I think I can not be mistaken in saying that his motives in the chief and crowning act of his life were highly patriotic and eminently self-sacrificing. Some evidences of this you will find in the Memorial I present to you; and as these sentiments were uttered in the unreserve and privacy of a correspondence never destined for the public eye, they will be accepted I think as truthful and sincere.

It may readily be conceived that as he was an only son, I was not without my visions of what the future might have in store for him. I can truly say, however, that I never indulged any extravagant expectations of his future eminence, for I never conceived him to be in any respect an extraordinary character. The crucial test of the Nation's agony suddenly brought to the surface qualities which before in a measure slumbered, a calm courage and a persistent devotion to the cause he had espoused, that although I might have conceived of their existence, I had not expected to see brought into such strong relief. A stern sense of duty was I think the ruling passion that carried him to the field and kept him there, while some others, superior to him in rank, and charged with far higher responsibilities, faltered and failed.

Some of my visions were associated with you and the scenes of that coming day when you will leave this your dear nursing mother to encounter the "dust and sweat" of the world's great theatre, where you too are to play your parts. In the mind's eye I saw him pass off this mimic stage to the broader field where men in the stern conflict of life contend for victory. If his taste and inclination had led him, as I had supposed they would, into the profession which his ancestors for three generations had pursued, I had thought that one of my occupations in the evening of life, now fast approaching, would be to guide in some measure his studies, to take him by the hand and lead him, as well as I knew how, to the "*apices juris*," the higher and the nobler walks of legal life, and shed upon his pathway, to the extent of my ability, something of that which

Lord Coke characterizes as "the gladsome light of jurisprudence." These visions are all ended—I will not say in grief and disappointment—for God had other purposes, and let me say far higher ends for him to accomplish, than could have been achieved by the most successful professional career. Although he was cut down upon the very threshold of manhood, with a character as yet but very imperfectly developed, he had his mission, which his Heavenly Father enabled him to accomplish.

> "That life is long that answers life's great end,"

says a high authority. By the grace of God he attained that end, and I am content. In the order of nature, and the usual allotments of Providence, I should long have preceded him to the grave. I shall not have the strong arm and the energetic will that I fancied in the coming days I might lean upon and confide in. I must look for him now beyond the stars, and if they who bear the cross shall inherit the crown, I may hope to meet him with the martyred host that have "come out of great tribulation, and have washed their robes, and *made them white in the blood of the Lamb.*"

I should do injustice to my own feelings, and a wrong to his memory, if I should fail to testify to the great goodness of our covenant God in the blessed assurance he permits us to entertain, that having honorably fulfilled his earthly mission, he has gone to his reward among the pure and the just in his Father's kingdom. Some of the evidences upon which this conviction is founded, will appear in the Memorial I present to you, while others have been conveyed to us in the narratives of loving friends, and from those to whom he unbosomed himself more freely in hours of sacred confidence. He was too truthful and sincere to make any declaration that he did not feel, and so distrustful of himself, and so anxious not to create an impression beyond the simple facts, that words from him on the subject of the higher relations of his being, had double power from the very reticence that restrained a fuller and ampler utterance. He died as he lived, full of love to all things beautiful and pure, bowing to his destiny with manly fortitude and resignation, with an unquenched patriotism that counted life as well lost in the cause of his country, and in the peace of his God and Saviour.

To many, may I not hope to all of you, my young friends, and especially to those who so recently, through the golden leaved gates of hope and faith, have, as you trust, entered into the kingdom of the Master, this assurance will be welcomed with high satisfaction. On the thirtieth of March last, my kind friend Professor North, who has done much to embalm the precious memory of WILLIE, wrote me a letter which contained the following sentence: "The death of three students who had enlisted for the war, has had something to do with the good work which God is doing in the College this Term." Of these students two were your classmates, him whom I have attempted to commemorate, and the other the bright, the noble, the heroic TURNER. This statement was to me most deeply interesting and affecting. There had been hours—I confess it with humiliation—during the past long and dreary winter, while the winds were howling their sad requiem over what seemed at such moments his untimely grave, when the cloud above my head was so dense and dark that I could not see even the silver lining that fringed it; but that simple fact drew aside the dark curtain, and through the rift in the cloud I saw the shining light and the throne all radiant beyond it, and as in a mirror I seemed to behold a new beauty in that life, and a wonderful significance in that death; and while I could ne'er forget, I less deplored my loss. Mysterious are the ways of Providence, more marvellous the pathway of the Spirit which can thus employ the red hand of war to guide the soul into God's perfect peace.

I place in each of your hands this little unpretending book. I do it with the hope that it may not only revive pleasant remembrances of your youthful friend, but that it may give you a higher estimate of the mighty conflict in which we are engaged. I do not urge you to follow him to the field where his young life was crushed out, but I do earnestly ask you to stand by the country and the Government, and by tongue and pen, by open testimony and by secret supplication you commend the great cause to the support of all honest and loyal hearts, and the favor and blessing of Almighty God. I shall follow you into life with interest strong and abiding in your welfare and success. May you each and all have grace to serve your generation in whatever useful or honorable career you may be called to act, to do something for your dear country in her hour of need, and much, very much, for truth and righteousness, and the building up and extension of the kingdom of Christ our Saviour; and when called hence, having fulfilled your earthly mission,

> "Pass through glory's morning gate,
> And walk in Paradise."

Mr. VAN NORDEN'S response was in these words:

DEAR SIR,—It seems to devolve on me to represent my classmates in expressing our sympathy for you in your bereavement, and our high appreciation of your kindness in supplying us with these tokens of our lamented classmate. You could not have presented to us a more acceptable gift. These Memorials will point us to facts and incidents concerning his earlier life and warlike experiences, of which we knew little. But, Sir, we needed no memorial. The image of WILLIE BACON is as fresh and clearly defined in our minds to-day, as when he left us for the army.

His open countenance and manly traits are too firmly fixed in our minds ever to be effaced by time. We remember him as he was when he entered College with us; we remember him as he was when he left us to fight the battles of his country; as the warrior-student we shall ever remember him.

We beheld him, dear sir, from a stand-point different from yours; but we feel that your parental affection and pride were not misplaced. Although he did not study hard during the short period of his collegate career, he stood high among his classmates.

He had a reserved power within him, which only needed study and training, or the quickening of some sudden emergency, to develop into mental acquirements and abilities of the highest order. He was no less distinguished for the nicety of his sensibilities, and the warmth and depth of his emotional nature, than for his intellectual gifts. Perhaps his most striking trait was his fearlessness. It adorned his countenanance, and beamed in his bold, dauntless eye. His ingenuousness was marked by every one. He was the soul of honor. No one can accuse him of ever having consciously done a mean or ungenerous thing. His courage, too, was noted by us all; and when in the hour of his country's dire need he hastened to her defense, we all felt that we had sent forth to the conflict a daring soul, who would not quail at the prospect of death itself. And we are assured now, that had his life been spared, his courage, his splendid talents, his restless energy, his all-absorbing devotion and high toned sensibilities would have, as they already had, insured him speedy promotion among his fellow officers.

And when the news flashed over the wires that WILLIE BACON had offered up his life on his country's altar—a willing sacrifice to freedom—that he had died whilst bravely leading his men into the thickest of the battle, our hearts were stricken with sorrow; but our grief was tempered with joy, for our own classmate had died the death of a hero. We would offer our heartfelt sympathy for your loss, but we at the same time congratulate you on being the father of such a son. Especially we rejoice with you, that in his dying hours he gave his heart to his Saviour; and that now, his battles fought, his victory won, he reigns in glory! Your loss—our loss—has been his gain! Sir, you have no cause for sorrow. Your son died a most enviable death. A manly soul, possessed of rare talents, full of generosity and ingenuousness, a martyr to freedom, his death is more glorious than the lives of many others. Henceforth he is enshrined in the hearts of all who knew him as one of our country's fallen heroes.

We thank you, sir, for these Memorials, these souvenirs of your beloved son, these tokens of your own good will. We accept them with gratitude. Be sure we shall preserve and esteem them as treasures. And throughout our lives we shall ever look back to WILLIE as one of the brightest jewels in the chaplet of our Alma Mater.

From the Cleveland (Ohio) Daily Herald of May 20, 1863.

A YOUNG SOLDIER'S GRAVE.

EDITORS OF THE HERALD,—

Will it be asking too much to request of you the publication of the following lines? A brief story will properly introduce them. Many hundred miles from here, in a quiet rural cemetery in Central New York, a young soldier sleeps, who gave all he had—his life—for his country. When the guns of traitors aimed at the starving garrison of Sumpter, startled the land, they found him at his books in an Eastern College. With the prompt instinct of patriotism, he dropped the toga of the scholar, and seized the sword of the volunteer. Wounded once, he returned again to the field, and in the first battle of Fredericksburgh fell a martyr to the holy cause he had with all the ardor of his nature espoused. His story is but one of a thousand which these sad and trying days are multiplying.

He was an only son, the central object around which the fondest affections and proudest hopes of his kindred were gathered. He sleeps, not where the foot of "the foe and the stranger will tread o'er his head," but where the hand of love can garnish his sepulchre.

One who loved him dearly, a few days ago placed upon his monument a bunch of pure white flowers, and returning from her pious errand, expressed the feeling of the moment in the following lines. They may, perchance, strike a responsive chord in some other stricken heart. C.

TO A WREATH OF WHITE FLOWERS ON WILLIE'S GRAVE.

Lie there upon his grave, pale lovely flowers,
  Mute emblems, all unconscious of your trust,
And yield your incense for a few short hours,
  Then die, above a hero's sacred dust.

Pure are your leaves, no shadows cloud their snows,
  No crimson flush, half hidden, hints of blame,
His stainless honor shames the fairest rose,
  No blemish soils the whiteness of his fame.

Your pale lips lie apart, your dying breath
  Flows out in delicate odors sweet and rare,
His memory breathes in blessing after death,
  Its heavenly fragrance haunts this earthly air.

Lie there, all helpless as he lies to-day,
  Frail trembling buds, nor heed the tears we shed,
Like him fear not to give your lives away,
  One more sad tribute to the early dead.

His fate and yours are one ;—fair stately flower,
  Cut down upon the land he could not save ;
His memory lends its sweetness for an hour,
  Then dies a guiltless offering on her grave.

UTICA, N. Y., *May* 12, 1863.

www.ingramcontent.com/pod-product-compliance
Lightning Source LLC
LaVergne TN
LVHW021431110826
845150LV00007B/2178

* 9 7 8 1 4 2 5 5 0 6 6 6 7 *